Across the Rim

to Ron, for guidance
to Morgan, for partnership
to Henry, for inspiration
to Mom, for love
to Dad, for care

ACROSS THE RIM

by Ben Folk

CONTENTS

Introduction to the Author

"Time is an illusion we have all wept and laughed. We exhaust ourselves with tales of predators and heroes. From time to time, a soul rises up not so much against the tide but rises up above it and thus becomes a master creator and illusionist while transcending this heated transom we call Planet Earth if not the entire physical universe.

It gives me great pleasure to introduce a gentleman of gentle bearing and strength, whose words surpass these illusions.

Ben Folk is such a writer and poet that his words are like stars that drift the night and twinkle at those who behold their meaning and emotional impact.

Furthermore, I have the additional pleasure to introduce you to Ben's fine volume of 30 poems. Ben not only will delight you with his words but the anecdotal notes at the end will provide refreshing post-introductions to each of the poems to further enhance your enjoyment. Each poem is followed by a set of notes. These notes portray the state of mind that the poet was experiencing prior to documenting it in poetic form."

- LARRY JAFFE, FLORIDA BEAT POET LAUREATE

Ship of Theseus

If you found the fragment stories of my life,
and pieced together these parts,
would you know me?

If I am becalmed in seas, long-dreaming,
replacing thoughts for driftwood,
I admit, I would become another to you
But ply away at my hull,
old age and misty fog banks,
shipwrecks from adventure
Would you not still know me
as I know myself?

Theseus!
Take away these boards
I do not need them
I will show my face as a sun of joy,
and others will feel warm
and know that we are alive
Is this not enough for you?

The trappings of Christmases and birthdays
A concerned look on a friend's face,
lost in a sea of uncertainty
How can you deny what you feel?

Worrying over broken planking floating in the tide
Do not remember me,
these puffs of smoke in the mind
Leave that for the undertow,
and be with me at every new day's dawn

NOTES

On my spiritual path, this was the first poem I wrote as my ability to be an artist was rehabilitated. It took me about 15 minutes to write, and was an absolute pleasure. I'm still very proud of it, and I enjoy it.

Theseus was a Greek hero who traveled around the isles and had many adventures.

In the world of academic philosophy, a lot of thought has been put into the problem of identity.

Rene DesCartes posited, "Cogito, ergo sum", "I think, therefore I am".

Without going too far into the nuances, even this seemingly incredibly simple statement has been picked apart by those with time on their hands to do so.

One philosopher pointed out this problem:

- Theseus got aboard his ship and went out on his adventures.

- As he went from port to port, his ship often needed repairs, and various parts were replaced by new wood and materials.

- By the time he returned home, not one piece of his ship was made of the original ship that launched when he started on his adventures.

- So…is this a new ship? Is it the same ship? How should we answer this question?

And the importance to this reader would be this: are you your memories? If you didn't have the pictures in your mind, would you cease to exist? Would you not know who you are anymore? Or is beingness something other than pictures, memories, planks, and driftwood?

Well, in my own personal spiritual renaissance, this question was answered.

And I wrote this poem.

BUDDHA

As I become less
I become more

As my own opinion
becomes nothing to me
I can understand
and appreciate yours
better

As I am not concerned
with me
I can more easily care
about you

As I feel less need
to assert my own view,
I am able to see,
and guide, and encourage
others

I can become us
only without myself

NOTES

I wrote this during 2020 because people were arguing. People who should know better, despite the circumstances, that fighting amongst each other, fighting for politics, fighting people with different viewpoints and calling them "evil", is always a losing game.

Beyond that, I was experiencing a tremendous spiritual transformation. I found that my beliefs, or really believing anything, was unimportant. I found it always limited my power, my ability to reach, and my ability to help.

For me, the self-discovery was that all my beliefs were created things, things I'd decided, and I found that they were all arbitrary.

A game (among other things) contains sides, viewpoints, decisions about the world. And I found that if I made a decision about how I view some part of the world, I was cutting away the rest of the world as "wrong".

And if I'd decided that part of the world was wrong, my approach to "help" that part of the world I disagreed with turned immediately to "harm" (or smash, extinguish, prove wrong, scoff at them, tell them to "get educated", etc.).

So the point is not totally "no one needs to believe anything," but more the idea that beliefs are subordinate to purpose, to what one is trying to do or get done.

If you feel that you've found the rules and boundaries to living a moral life, there is a tendency to notice that others have not made this same discovery, and so conclude that they are living an "immoral life".

But if you want to help them, this conclusion will likely cloud that help, prevent one from granting beingness to another, a tendency to ignore their agency, and forget their spiritual nature.
I saw a lot of disgust during 2020.

So I wrote this poem.

NATIVE

I have often asked my Father for counsel
He has seen many things,
and many people
And he has been many things,
and many people

I have not always understood him
But being his Son,
I know he has never lied to me

One day I asked him why this was;
and he told me these seven lessons,
which are one lesson:

The truth when dying is Death

The truth when afraid is poison

The truth when angry is battle

The truth when bored is unimportant

The truth when happy is encouragement

The truth when peaceful is love

The truth when God is to Be

NOTES

The wild thing about the truth, or at least what we feel is true at any given time, is that it seems to always be filtered through a wavelength, through how we feel.

But our viewpoint, to us, always seems to be the end all, be all truth. Which is nonsense. It's a truth from a viewpoint. And I've wondered - does the bully see himself in all the movies that show how awful a bully is? Does he know that's him? Or can he not afford self-reflection?

So when we are full of hate for the person that prescribes adderall to children, we might think or even say, "Those people should be destroyed!". And while it is a very understandable viewpoint, it isn't what we would consider true when we are experiencing our most profound spiritual states.

And, it seems, as a person is able to move freely through different viewpoints, and comes to see for themselves that there are in fact different viewpoints, they can more clearly judge their own statements.

All these levels of truth and viewpoint are relative, all except the last one. "The truth when God is to Be" simply states that everything exists, that there is no conflict despite apparencies, and it can show upon reflection that every statement below it contains one or more lies and are not truly true.

But go ahead and try to end all games for a person and they will, by and large, try to fight you. So while it may be a useful truth for an individual, it may not have as much workability in trying to teach, assert, or enforce this on another.

It brings to mind this very fun four lines:

Seeker: What is the secret to happiness?

Master: To not argue with fools.

Seeker: I disagree.

Master: Yes, you are right.

REBIRTH

I have no clear memory
of the moment you pulled me from the salty sea
I, barely conscious
You, full of focus
Both of us gasping for breath

I knew nothing of sailing
But I remember you kneeling next to me,
hand extended, pointing the way,
instructing me in everything I had forgotten;
things I'd need to know
for the time you'd be gone

For so much of our journey,
through calms and storms,
I clung to your legs,
trying to remember who I was
amidst those skirts

Maybe you fell once or twice
into the sea
And maybe I was there for you
I honestly don't remember
So often I was simply worried for myself,
as many a wave
seemed taller than my spirit

But there did come a day
when land was at last in sight
And having learned the lessons of the sea,
you went ashore and climbed the banks,

pulled stones from the high beach,
and stacked tall, unmoving walls,
floor of sand, roof of thatch;
Nothing like a ship deck

I cannot say what drew me back to the waters
I have never liked the sea
Maybe there was simply not enough room
amongst the stones

More likely you knew:
nothing essential returns
harbored on a shore,
or resting beneath the sun

And so, paddling against the tides
under your watchful eye,
I ventured out to reclaim my memory,
maybe deep in the ocean,
or perhaps in another sea

NOTES

I wrote this about my mom and me.

Here are the spoiler notes.

The first stanza is about being born, birth.

The second stanza sums up, for me, my mom's incredible willingness to give to me. She poured so much care and instruction into me, pointing things out, explaining things to me, orienting me to the world I was in. It also alludes to me (and all of us) having lived before with the "forgotten" concept. The situation of being a child, having amnesia as a spirit, and just being severely disoriented makes life very hard, and very interesting.

Fourth, more allusion to having lived before.

The fifth was very poignant for me. This is when my mom moved into the time of her life near retirement, and into retirement. She and her husband built a very idyllic scene for themselves. They had worked very hard in life and robustly enjoyed life after work (though they still worked, in a sense, very physically active, tending to 35 acres of property, building gardens and structures. However, the tall stones also represent a tombstone, the final building pieces.

Sixth, seventh, and eighth, if my mom didn't love me so much, she would have just invited or allowed me to come live with them. It wasn't until I was 35 years old that I started to succeed at anything in life. I didn't like the struggle, I was still confused and didn't understand much. But she pushed me, kept me facing life, didn't allow me to just live on her couch and, eventually, I made something of myself, and I was so very happy to make her proud.

Also...

"as many a wave seemed
taller than my spirit"

I've never liked these lines. They feel too cliche. But there they are, still in the poem.

THE FOLDS

Hundreds of years ago
the now legendary smiths from Japan
realized the swords they made
for the Samurai,
whose lives depended
on quality craftsmanship,
were breaking on the battlefield
due to impurities in the steel,
mostly in the form of carbon

One smith, Akumi,
developed the now famous process
of folding steel

Through heat and precision hammering,
the impurities were driven out

But, in the process,
something astonishing was discovered:
folding a blade ten times
created more than a thousand layers
in the steel,
making the sword nearly indestructible...

In more modern times
we've been shown
the size of the sun,
the distance to the moon,
we've been told the number of years
across the galaxy,
the light we'll never catch

And so we are made to feel
so small,
that we have become
almost nothing

But

you should see what happens
when you try to fold a piece of paper
eight times...

The miracle,
the literal explosion
of geometric progression

It only takes folding a piece of paper
45 times
to reach the moon
81 folds
to span the Andromeda galaxy
103 folds
to span the breadth
of the entire known universe

So while some continue to perfect
the art of war,
seeing if they can show others
how small and mortal
they'd like them to feel,
others seek to perfect
the recovery of the spirit,
folding ourselves,
pressing out the impurities,
and, in realization, come to know
we are not a carbon based lifeform

Instead, we find ourselves
folded, expanded,
standing on the doorstep of everything

NOTES

You are not your body.

You are a spiritual being, and you may happen to have a body.

A huge number of people in this world think they are an animal, and would narrow that down to the idea that they are their brain, or that their consciousness is stored in their brain.

Yet they always say "my brain" with the idea that it is an owned tool, and is not them.

This is the same way the Christian will often say "my spirit", but the idea really is "me". But even the Christian is sold to some degree that they are a body.

The scientist, and science-minded people often push very hard on the idea that you are a body. To me, there is almost a kind of hysteria beneath the surface in their need for you to accept you are a body.

But you are not. And neither are they.

But it is understandable. We do in many ways seem to be a body. We don't necessarily know if animals are anything but bodies. Maybe some are, and maybe some aren't. I guess the same could be considered for human beings.

Perhaps many, or even most, or even all animals are in fact bodies. Biological machines.

But I am not, and you are not, and the atheist is not.

We are creators. There may be an ultimate God. There may not be. It could be you are God, it could be we are God, it could be any number of things.

But the most important first step toward anything, quite literally anything and everything in life, is the discovery that you are not your body.

Because it's not something I or anyone can tell you that will make it so.

It's experienced by you, found out by you, just like it was experienced and found out by me.

But the scientist seems to have an impulse to show you that you are basically nothing because you are so small. A body.

And even the modern spiritualist today takes hallucinogens to try to induce a spiritual state.

What he is actually doing is one of two things - scrambling his mind so badly that he disorients himself as a spirit so thoroughly that he momentarily exteriorizes, or he is poisoning his body so badly that he momentarily exteriorizes as the body moves toward death.

But the approach of drugs or hallucinogens is just more agreement that you are a body. Using matter to disrupt matter in order to shake the spirit loose will not lead to a solution.

In fact, it is likely to lead to heavier need of the drug because the desire to induce the state will grow stronger.

And that is because there is, in fact, freedom.

Expression

I looked up from my work,
writing important messages,
looked out a window and saw,
very high in the sky
a swirl of clouds
moving perfectly
to a wind that existed
in a place no human being
would ever touch,
and I thought,

"Why is that happening?
Why is that doing that,
since no sentience
will ever experience or touch it?
Is it doing that because
a butterfly flaps its wings?
If it doesn't do that,
will a man forget
to go to a grocery store
and pick up flowers for his wife,
and will this lead
to a child never being born?"

And I wondered at the girl
on the other side of the galaxy,
looking perhaps at water
going down a storm drain,
and wondering the same thing

Do solar systems
also look like swirling clouds?

Do I?

And then I paused to write this down

NOTES

This is simply a description of what happened one moment during a day at work.

It is currently popular to wonder at how small and insignificant mankind is, how small the individual life is, how we are all animals, how big the universe is, how important science is, and how real physics is.

I think this is just a method of lessening the pressures in the mind - the stored physical, emotional, and spiritual pain of the eons, the painful amnesia that grips nearly every human being on Earth that compels us to examine matter, the atom, ad infinitum, to see if we can ever find out who we are and why we're here.

On the contrary, I believe we are all connected, that the individual is all-encompassing and infinite, and that the experiences and existence of any being is all there really is, and that the rest, including the physical universe, is merely invention.

So I took a moment to write this poem.

PELICAN

I watched a pelican hunt,
hovering above the shallow shore

Small fish swam there,
these daring to seek the plants
and smaller life comprising their food

The plants there,
daring to grow in the shallows,
in the heated waters
of the Floridian sun

A second pelican joined,
but no more plants could grow
to feed more fish
to support more than the pair,
all locked in a mortal coil

Later, I wept while staring at a painting
The colors and abstract splashes
mirrored ancient joy
in the seat of my soul

The artist, a woman unknown to me
had tiptoed her way
across the galactic rim
choosing a little of this, and a little of that,
whimsically, knowingly

She expected not
that this one expression
should sound the bell of every man
But that some should hear it
and weep
And that others would wait their turn,
some with the breath of anticipation,
some with souls so dead
that only scant few remained
who could guess the secret combination
that might stoke the fires
of their creativity once again

And so they wait for her
like stones
in shallow water

NOTES

This is one of my only poems where the title is in the poem. It's a personal preference. The title can be its own "one-liner", or it can be a very high conceptual description that will invite further thought once the reader is done reading.

But for this one, I was watching pelicans. And I liked the title "Pelican", as it makes it kind of mysterious...I guess it wasn't all that mysterious.

Anyhow, I hope you liked the poem. Here's bluntly what it was about from my perspective as the writer.

1. Animals (like pelicans), and those physical and biological entities and systems, are locked into a finite circumstance.

2. Spiritual beings are not, and can create effects beyond matter, energy, space, and time; a spiritual being can violate the Laws of Thermodynamics.

The changeover in the middle, from pelican to painting, may come across a bit jarring. It was intended that way. Maybe it was too much, but I like it.

The spirit creates the universe.

If the examination of the universe only leads one to finding more universe, then one is heading the wrong direction. This is what most science is doing. The scientist who is also an artist (or vice versa) is the one who will find themselves eventually.

THE FOUNTAIN

We ask each other to be like the other,
that gravity-strong desire,
so we can know one another

But onward we go, always parallel,
watching and wishing
Even clothed in the trappings of Rome
each off us secretly knows: I have resisted

And having hidden our secret rebellion
in a box, in a box, in a box,
so that when I beseech you,
please, conform and mirror this dance,
even you cannot hear your own scarlet laughter
echoing through your mind
like the windchimes of outer space
hidden from all sight, only to release
on death

Yet I still implore you
to change the smile of Mona Lisa
because I am so blind to even my own artistry
that I never noticed how we move
through a maelstrom of postulates
Neptune's grip, guiding us down to stillness,
some dimly-lit, pre-determined path

So we brace ourselves
against these wind-swept barriers,
encased in invisible stone
clutching our hammer and chisel —
do we continue our cave etchings?

Or can we break free,
tools falling, prison vanishing,
and cascade in spirals of electric color
across the universe,
dying fireworks, born again to new expression

Set in motion by love,
by Mechanus,
by The Creator,
by ourselves

NOTES

I think many of us have a shared, upsetting experience with life.

We can't understand why a person would think or behave the way we do.

Those who live a shallow life just leave it at that. They just think someone or something (a person, a movie, etc.) is stupid or weird and they move on, just a bit disturbed or upset.

Then there are many who are like, no, wait, why in the heck is this happening? How can that person think or behave that way? Don't they see? Don't they get it?

And, for me, personally, as I kept having this experience and trying to get at the root of it, I settled on this:

I want everyone to be like me, or at least very, very close to the same as me.

I want a harmonious universe.

And when harmony goes very out of whack, it has disturbed me.

The the truth, of course, is, that each of us is about as unique as it gets. The uniqueness of each of us is actually so absolute (in my experience) that it's a real miracle that we are here together at all sharing any kind of experience. The uniqueness is so strong that sometimes I actually wonder if, in fact, you exist at all, or, if possibly, everyone and everything are just made up in my head, my own creations, that occasionally do disturbing things to keep things interesting. I create, have harmony, intentionally forget, get some disharmony, am shocked, and then have to re-discover what's going on.

Or maybe you do exist, but we're still doing essentially that activity of re-discovery.

And the uniqueness is first captured in the poem with the line:

"But onward we go, always parallel…"

And expressing the anguish we sometimes have to change another from their own unique expression to something we can understand easier:

"Yet I still implore you to change the smile of Mona Lisa"

And the line about "in a box" is just a guess at how we trick ourselves into not understanding what's happening. If you were playing three-card Monte, but against just yourself, how many switches would you have to make until you actually forgot which card was the queen?

"Mechanus" is simply the physical universe, or possibly just the representation of orderliness. For anyone who has played Dungeons & Dragons, the inspiration was from Primus, ruler of Mechanus.

The interesting thing is that, recognizing that everyone is unique, and then truly living with that fact, are two different things.

I'm very glad for my spiritual path in that regard. It has improved things dramatically and continues to do so. I am able to love so many more people than I used to.

FULCRUM

He was wild,
exhausted and hungry,
lost across space and time,
out of place and sorts
And so was I

His small body turned
pirouetting, he spun, eyes distant
I only wanted to leave
and he claimed to want only to stay
He fought me, resisted,
raised his voice with incoherent words
and unlearned grammar

I filled my lungs with breath,
fury gathering, to be let loose
Instead, I lost consciousness

And the galaxy spun,
drifting at speeds I could never know
Planets, clinging at the edges to simply hang on
My own lifeforce, I felt it,
tethered to the uncountable numbers
that had come before me
I felt the lives that existed on distant planets,
all their comings and goings,
fireflies at sundown
The black holes
collected at the center of the galaxy
reached out, clawed at me, tugging
My own mind, I could feel it

rage with life, and part of it, an ancient evil
filled with the pain of every birth and every loss,
it snapped with electricity
crackled as it settled, and then beat at my brain
like an ocean tide of heat and cold
and out of it came the slap of the open hand
of my great great great grandmother
whistling at me again and again
Words shouted in numb disappointment

And also God touched me
through every conduit we have ever known,
every true messiah, every hero
I felt them with me
wondering what I would do next

And when I came to,
I found him in my arms
His shoulders gripped in my hands
his face
wondering what I would do next

NOTES

I have seen children mistreated.

I've seen their personalities blunted, their happiness squashed, their energy diminished. All by parents who do not understand children, themselves, life, or really anything.

I wanted to write a poem about a parent who is suddenly thunderstruck by the visceralness of the entire universe, knocked so hard by their interconnection with the existence of everything, including the dread truth of their own past, that it would give them pause before mistreating their own child.

That is all this poem is about. We would have world peace in one generation if all parents ceased to mistreat their children.

THE MIRROR

Shall we say he was not loved?

Conceived in silent darkness
An accident
of sexual frustration

Swaddled to mother's warmth
Clanking dishes
Whisk of broom

Father's hands rough on his face,
peeling like thin ribbons
from laying wet concrete

Toddling in an empty house
Repurposed objects for toys
Silence, clanks, silence, whisks

Safety runs in a pack of boys
Marauding, chained or unchained,
the only rule to ownership is "take"

Mother somehow never saw
the bright red bike
half-tucked under the stoop

Father's time on Sunday
Ambivalent questions and a catch
between downs and beers

Teachers waiting every day,
whole classrooms silent,
seeing if he has the right words

Whether he fled or was told to leave
camouflaged he went
graduating from violence to violence
formerly scorned, now condoned

But was he not loved?
Is football love?
Is a clean house love?
Did any teacher ever commend him
even when he was small?

Given nothing real from the world
that he might become
and reflect back, brighter,
need we even call him human?
Or is he only an echo
fading down the family tree?

Regimented, sharpened, toughened
Delivered across the sea
Lockstep marching,
clanks, whisks, questions, silence,
to the open field of battle
only to hear
the ring of a gunshot
hang in the air
and die
in another man's country

NOTES

There are about 350,000,000 people in the United States at the time of this writing.

11.6 percent are in poverty.

Poverty is defined as a household income that is insufficient to purchase basic needs.

That's about 1 out of every ten people in our country cannot afford basic needs.

When I look around my neighborhood, and outlying neighborhoods, I don't think there's a single person in poverty.

That means they are elsewhere, potentially packed together by the hundreds or thousands.

I wouldn't know, I've never directly seen it.

Now, there are whole books, philosophies, political beliefs, and ways and viewpoints on life that do not empathize with this kind of thing. And I tend to lean toward that category - I don't believe there is a single victim in the whole wide world, never has been, never will be. We have the word "victim", we have the concept for it, but my belief is that it is total fiction. Like nearly every-thing, it's an invention to describe something, maybe a feeling, maybe a sense of fairness or justice.

But from my own personal viewpoint, when I look at life from the spiritual side of things, I don't find any truth or any real usefulness in the concept of a victim.

That said, I can and do empathize. I can get into the story of it. In my heart, if I were to lose my son before I myself passed, well I don't know if I would survive long. And if I did, I don't really know...I'll just leave it at that.

This poem is about the neglected child, the young man who grows up with parents that don't truly love children. With teachers that don't have the ability or willingness to ensure every student makes it.

When I was in my 20's, I went to the east coast, Baltimore, and sold educational books door-to-door. I went into poor or low-middle class communities, knocked on doors, and met people.

One day, I was walking through a neighborhood (I had no car or mode of transportation), and I came across a boy and his friends and I asked them for directions. They told me where to go and asked what I was doing. I told them, and one of the boys gave me his bike and told me to keep it, that I needed it, and that he didn't mind.

I was blown away. Such generosity!

But here's the truth: that bike was stolen. And I was so ignorant of life and circumstances that I thought I'd just run across the most generous young man in the whole world.

"Safety runs in a pack of boys
"Marauding, chained or unchained,
the only rule to ownership is "take""

This poem is also about war.

We send children to war. We send our little ones to war. That's who is going to war.

That's who is the "Army of One" or whatever PR campaign is currently being run to sell the idea that it's responsible, successful, moral, good, or whatever else, to join the ranks of those who protect our country.

Or those children who are then delivered into the hands of those politicians or political interests, or money-making war machines that have decided there's a terrorist to kill, or is that oil to take.

Or whatever. It doesn't really matter.

Our children are being put under the command of those who are better than them, know better than them, and have intel "you just wouldn't understand because the world is more complex and more dangerous than you could possibly know."

Yeah, well, you get exactly what you put your attention on.

Now, again, for me, no victims. Not the children, not the parents, not me, not you.

But I really don't like that game. And I think we should stop, wholesale.

I do believe there are tremendously evil men and women in the world. I do think some of these people are in power, or influence power. And I don't think these people should be rooted out, be made known, and be prevented from taking any position in society. I don't think they should be executed, but I do feel they are the ones that should be living in government housing, and fed and clothed by the grace of the vast majority who only want good things for themselves, and their sons and daughters.

But the game of sending our children to die, far away from home, for a cause and purpose they've been told that is mostly or entirely a lie, should end.

That is not love.

THE TOWER

I believe in you
From long ago and far away, I believe in you
If you are reading this, I believe in you

Your goodness
Your desire to be kind
Your hope that all will be well again

Your expression of you is important
Others see you
And I believe in you

And, together, we can believe in others
We can see through their anguish
And we can call it stupidity, or even insanity

But we can also believe in them
Together we can expand
And believe

Though they may lash out
And talk of a burning planet
Prisoners wrapped in self-immolation

You and I
We can believe
Until they are ready

NOTES

This poem represents the current culmination of my expression of love for the people of this world.

My own personal belief system has taken an extremely pleasant 180 degree turn as I've moved through my spiritual path.

I used to be a hardcore Self-Determined Objectivist - right and wrong, black and white, prove it to me, only the facts, we cause our future through key decisions we make each and every day, etc., ad nauseum.

Now I'm very much a Subjectivist who leans heavily toward what looks like Fatalism - I create literally every experience I have, it's questionable if there's a universe outside of my experiences at all, I don't commit to the idea that anything unobserved exists, and I think that my entire experience of the universe through all time was known by me prior to any of it happening and that I'm basically shrinking myself to a tiny sliver of time in order to experience things like emotions - like jumping into the film of a movie while it's playing.

So I can afford to love others. I can afford to not judge their actions with even a shred of harshness.

My experience so far has been that there is unbelievable personal power in belief. In self, in others, in circumstances.

On the other hand, if someone harmed my son I might kill them. So while it might be true that we actually exist outside the bounds of space and time, I reserve my right to be a participant in this film in whatever manner I see fit.

And I reserve that right for you as well.

SPOTTING SPOTS

I remember the day
I realized I had only ever talked to
a made up creation of you
in my mind

Profound understanding of this golem,
carefully crafted from the gray clay
in my skull

But one evening, while quite exhausted
and deciding to go to bed,
I found myself looking
at the tiniest stitch on my couch,
perfectly joined, tied amongst
thousands of similar
but different
stitches

And as I started then to notice
the uniqueness of everything,
the breath in my lungs in that moment,
that tick, of my watch, right then,
and realizing it was likely that

no one

had ever looked at that stitch before,
that I was the first, and likely the last,
to ever look at that stitch

I started to feel a pleasant vertigo
of the threads of my mind
coming apart
coming untangled

I no longer saw a body, a past, a set of decisions, scars, attitudes, sexuality, a face, a
mind, neurons, electricity, particles, atoms

What I had left, was you
And the feeling of wondering
what you might do or say next

And as I was finally free to meet you,
I could now meet others,
and I could know myself,
and finally meet God

NOTES

We often treat people like they are a set of behaviors.

We treat them like they are the collection of actions they've done in the past.

We do this because we want to feel safe, secure. It just wouldn't do to have big, powerful beings walking around doing whatever they wished, whenever they wished it, unpredictable, unchained, able to create anything.
So we keep a voodoo doll of them in our heads, stitched together by the patterns we've observed them do, the spiderweb patterns we pray they stay stuck in.

And so we talk to the constructs in our heads, rarely ever really talking to anyone. Instead, we talk to a bunch of (we hope) predictable phrases. And then we repeat our same nonsense phrases over and over again with our fingers crossed that everyone will just keep. saying. the same. things.

But anytime we like, if we'd like to actually meet someone, and feel alive, we can stop talking to those made up collections in our minds.

THE SONG OF ABRAHAM

Had I been dead to life so long?
Selfish self, hoarding time
Castaway with nothing
but calm ocean and sun,
bidding farewell
to the shores of Creation

Yet thank the Lord of All
for her gentle breath
sending my raft across the sea
to new beach, new sand
And there she delivered a son

His first breath, and mine
Resurrected, I built a house
before the treeline –
wary of dark jungles, desirous
to devour my new joy

"Bring him out! Bring him out!
"Give him over to needles, pills, and rifles
"Bring him to the mount, strike him down!
"Submit his body to war
"Throw it on the ashes of history books,
"for other children to learn what happened,
but never to read his name"

And seeing this, and hearing well,
fear settled on my waking thoughts and
disturbed my nightly rest
For though spirit, immortal be,
imagination may dream of endless death

And as I stood before the trees,
listening to the echoed words,
a gentle breeze came again,
and I was pulled once more
from cast off places

Now with only rustling leaves,
I knelt before my son and said:
"You will live beautifully, if you wish it
"Your sword, clean hands
"Your shield, a clear mind
Your armor, to love despite all"

And these three gifts given,
I stood and turned again
to face the shadowed wood
bordering the sand

And feeling the ebb and flow,
the tides of love and dread
criss-cross my universe in scintillating light,
I watched his first steps
and prayed, as every father does,
that we would meet,
and always meet again,
on the open beach of home

NOTES

God decided to test the faith of Abraham.

He told him to take his son to the mount, and sacrifice him.

Abraham proceeded to do God's will.

At the last moment, as Abraham was about to strike the blow, and Angel stayed his hand.

Abraham had passed the test of faith.

I think the account is both horrible and beautiful, and there are many thoughts, emotions, topics, and parallels to life that come out of it.

Near the end of my first marriage, I got a vasectomy. I had no plans to have children, and no particular desire to do so. I enjoyed the company of kids, enjoyed playing with them and entertaining them, but had no desire to become a father.

Then I got divorced, and a couple years later got married again, and my wife wanted children. She knew I'd had a vasectomy, and we'd looked up getting it reversed, so we knew it wasn't a sure thing and we were prepared for however it went.

I told her I still had no desire to have kids, but that I would be fine if we did have kids, and I would love them and be responsible for them.

Then I crossed a major threshold on my spiritual journey.

And I remember the moment, sitting in my office, and noticing some emotion deep inside of me had suddenly come alive. Just a flicker. But it was love. It was knowing that I was going to become a dad, and that I would have a child, and I felt love.

My wife wasn't even pregnant yet. I just knew I was going to be a dad. And I wept with joy.

So I got the vasectomy reversed, the procedure worked, and we had our son, Henry.

Many father's talk about that first moment, that something happens to them, something unsuspected and often overwhelming.

And that's what happened to me. Joy and gratitude the likes of which I hadn't felt before and haven't felt since.

Henry is five at the time of this writing, and that feeling is with me every single day.

I love my wife, I love my mom, and I love my sister. All of them, deeply.

But I love Henry in a way that is different. It's not "more", it's different. It's sacrificial.

It manifests in the highest of pleasures. But it's also kept me up many nights worrying about his health, potential accidents, intruders to our house that I might have to murder, cars I'd throw myself in front of, and on. And on. And on.

Henry will never attend public school. There is too much interest in our society, from parents, kids, teachers, administrators, to create victims of children, to suggest drugs for behavior, and to validate insanity and actually push or celebrate the pain in the mind that manifests in people as illness of body or character.

He will never have victimhood as something he should aspire to.

He will never have "being a soldier" as something he must admire.

And while he will absolutely have to contend with the insanity of this world, I will arm him as we go, step by step, so he is oriented to what he is seeing.

The love...the dread...

So far, so good. So far, so good.

INQUISITION

He asked me to explain myself,
was it this or was it that
What are my ethics

How can I explain life,
a quantum experience
that gives yes and no
simultaneously?
One electron
alight in two spaces

Maybe I agreed with you
until you observed me
Or maybe it was until
you asked your question

Life is not explained
It is not even observed
It is only experienced

Even your anger is only the tiniest,
almost immeasurably small
expression of you

Because when the scientist looks,
he discovers you both hate
and love me
at the same time

And so perceiving, he ascends
out of delusion
into mystery,
far below knowing

NOTES

I don't actually believe life is a quantum experience.

But I do believe people don't want you to change your mind.

When you say something, there seems to be a decided need in nearly everyone for you to stay with that decision, that it must become part of your character, something they can rely on.

And people want you to have reasons for everything. Why do you think what you think?

But the odd truth is, that nearly all reasons will go back to something like, "because I like that", or "because I decided that". Something like that will be the basic on almost every opinion, thought, idea, or action.

And my opinion is that this is because you are a spiritual being that is entirely at cause, and causing things, at all times. I think that is literally all you do. And reasons are just complexities we build on top of these things in order to have arguments on the internet. And, also more seriously, to have the game of getting to know each other.

But "having reasons" is also a favored trap for the weak, the coward, and the person with ill intentions. They use your own reasons to pin you into being something, admitting to something, siding with something, etc., ad infinitum. Just a trap by those people, all the way down.

But here's the real thing here - I reserve the right to change my mind for any reason, and for no reason, at any time, and for any length of time, and to change it back, or to anything else, whenever I choose.

And I recommend the same for you and everyone else as well.

It will make you the most free, and the most powerful.

The Pillars of Eternity

For those alive in Bedlam, heed these words:

1. Let no man hate with certainty, for he is always wrong

2. Invoke not possessing knowledge of God, for those who live in the finite assign only false things to the infinite

3. Pretend not to secret and hidden knowledge, for it is secret and hidden by definition

4. Know that evil exists, but focus on it not lest ye become it

5. Spread not thine enemy's message, for ye will soon find it everywhere

6. Belief that another man is thine enemy is poor judgment, for all are but a mirror

7. Accept the observations of another as fact at thy greatest peril, for ye are alive in Bedlam

NOTES

The world we live in is not "the result of natural forces or nature".

People's behavior here (and my opinion is sweeping and almost total) is not sane, rational, or even natural.

First, there is a very small segment of people, in all walks of life, who have constant and continuous destructive intentions for those around them and the world at large.

These people effectively poison others around them to adopt similar behaviors.

The rest of us have been hamstrung by the collected physical and emotional pain in our mind from this current lifetime, as well as all our previous lifetimes, that we now essentially are unable or even refuse to see, face, confront, and do something about those who are destroying and harming others.

It's there. We sense it. We, by and large, say and do nothing.

And so we live in Bedlam. An insane asylum.

In talking about another poem, I claimed that if everyone in the world loved their children, we'd have world peace in one generation. Because of the above, that isn't actually true. Resolving the above two things (those with perpetual destructive intentions, and our own painfully crushed spirits) are required in my opinion for any true peace in the world.

During 2020, during Covid, I wrote this poem.

There were a lot of acquaintances, and even some friends of mine, who seemed to be going insane.

One of the first things I noticed was that some segment claimed to have access to a government agency at the highest of clearance levels who went by the moniker, "Q".

My wife told me about this "Q", and I asked her point blank, "Do the people who are into this know that it's probably some 15 year old from Reddit pranking them?"

She said no.

I then looked into who among my friends was claiming access to this "Q", and a profile seemed to emerge.

It looked pretty clear that the folks who were into it, interested in it, even hyper fixated on it, were people who did not have a strong grasp of technology or the internet. They hadn't grown up with the technology, hadn't really seen how it worked, weren't totally aware of the kinds of personalities that were online, weren't really aware of platforms like Twitter where anonymous profiles would spew endless hate, unchecked, because they were anonymous.

They didn't track.

And Q told them a story. And it was a story they'd been wanting to hear for a long time.

And from that, I watched one segment of people start to strongly hate another segment of people.

I watched some stand on their spiritual beliefs and point out how soulless others were.

Q gave them all very hidden and secret knowledge.

They focused on it, devouring it, and it started to devour them.

They began to spread the message, and moved to other more "free" platforms so they could "talk openly" about the secrets and the coming storm.

They never noticed that when you elect another your enemy, you also to that degree admit that you are an enemy of yourself.

All of the above also applies to the other side of the fence to the Black Lives Matter community.

The concept of Q had some tremendously admirable aspects to it, and much of the story that was pushed about the evils and corruption of the government, likely had a lot of truth in it. And then it went south. Quickly.

The concept of BLM was beautiful. I even publicly explained that the concept was a good thing and what reason people had to be making that statement. I was immediately attacked by a number of people, and I removed my statement after some discussion. But the concept itself was and is beautiful. And then it went south. Quickly.

And as to the last one, #7, the one I personally consider the most important, the one I live by - never, under any circumstances, ever believe you have "the facts" based on what someone else said. The only fact you have is that someone else made a statement. It may or may not be true. You can act on it as though it is fact. But incorporating it into your own personal catalog of facts?

Well, do so at your greatest peril, for ye are alive in Bedlam.

The Things We Tell Ourselves

She held my hand
while we put each of my stories
through the paper shredder

"I'm unlucky and there are no opportunities"
An old favorite
So much worry! So much envy of others!

Maybe I could hang onto it for just a little longer...
Instead, I reached for it, dropped it in!
Bbbbrrrrrr!!!

I panicked as the story was destroyed!
But then, an enormous relief

And suddenly, I solved the riddle
of how to attract and have
what I wanted in life
I was lucky,
and there were opportunities

I felt like a God

She squeezed my hand tightly,
giving me an encouraging, but nervous smile

I reached for another, and then another
"Why can't people be more like me?"
"I'm smarter than everyone else"

"I can't balance work and life"
The particle dust of the paper,
the heat of the machine,
and the now satisfying "Bbbbrrrrrr!!!"
filling the air

We danced and shredded,
laughed tears of relief and shredded,
and after some while
I found I was looking
at the last of my stories

"Save the girl"

The piece de resistance
of my entire character and personality
The motivating force of my life

How could I let this go?
So much love...
So much pain...

She no longer squeezed my hand,
she looked neither at me, nor my story
She looked away,
as if interested in something
on the far horizon,
giving me the privacy
to do what needed to be done

So I picked it up and
dropped it in

NOTES

Our lives, and the stories of our lives can be beautiful. And they can be a trap.

They can be a trap in that one may forget, or not realize, they're just making up the importances of things as they go along, and this produces emotions, and that is part of the reward for living the story.

If you realized you were just making things up and telling yourself something, the emotion might be less impactful, less juicy, and you might lose interest.

Another oddity is the equality of human problems.

I've had a job where, in the office in which I worked, filling out a certain series of documents was a really big deal, a big task, a headache, something people rolled their eyes at and made jokes about.

I've also had a job where the entire income of the company, the jobs and livelihood of some 40 people, was dependent on me, my actions, my success or failure, every single week.

And there are people with stakes much higher than the ones I've had that I've named here.

A religious minister might feel that he has the most important job in the entire world, the one with the most at stake. If he succeeds in his dissemination, he wins spiritual freedom for others, or heaven, or Nirvana. If he fails, a being stays in a torturous trap, hell, or the karmic wheel continues to grind them down.

I've actually had all three of the above jobs — administrator, salesperson, religious minister. And the emotions connected to the problems associated with each job were, by and large, almost identical in feeling of weight and consequence.

Clearly they aren't the same. But that's how they felt.

The interesting thing for me on my spiritual path has been — the stories I've been telling myself my whole life, and for eons, have largely dissolved.

I still have plenty of emotions. I still play at the game of life, and I still win and lose.

But it has been interesting to become more and more of a player who knows he is playing.

It's been the difference between being locked into games I had no idea I was creating, and creating new games in my life to play and find out what happens.

For a long time, most of my life, I thought what I wanted was no game at all. I wanted peace. I didn't necessarily just want to become a trillionaire and rule everything, but I just felt I didn't want the barriers, the emotions, the upsets. And I thought I was willing to sacrifice happiness if I could somehow achieve that. I thought that I wanted zero.

But what I've found is that I wanted out of a trap I was in. And the trap was a massive collection of games I was playing in the background and running on repeat.

But as I've recovered myself more and more, spiritually, I've recovered my ability to create, to be an artist, to act out of duty, and to love others.

"And that has made all the difference."

– ROBERT FROST

LOVE
(FOR MORGAN)

We measure intentions by weeks,
the thoughts we pour in,
what we give of ourselves

We measure thoughts by depth,
a love with steady expansion,
a beacon for others

We measure love by strength,
and the Bridges we cross
hand in hand

NOTES

I wrote this for my wife.

She prefers short poems.

So I packed our life and love as well as I could into three short stanzas.

She loved it.

FOR HENRY

Nearly everyone you talk to
or will ever meet
is sound asleep

Nearly everything almost everyone
says and does
is based on something from the past

from the past
from the past
from the past

You will mistake manic joy
(and other things)
for real joy
(and other things)
You will say, "They are so happy!"
and you will be wrong

You will trust
when you need to guide
You will feel dismay
when you need to feel compassion
You will be surprised
when you need to understand

But as long as you remember this lesson
you will recover
and learn
and grow

NOTES

My son's name is Henry, and I wrote this for him when he was four years old.

One of the greatest points of human suffering I've observed is when a person fails to understand another person.

That failure is based largely from not observing or knowing what is actually going on with other individuals, and failing to notice where one is and what's going on in the environment.

Television, movies, politics, and many other things put forward an impression of "what's normal".

All these things are missing fundamental truths about the mind and spirit.

And so a "social facade" is created And the truth is nearly everyone is wearing a nearly endless series of masks at all times.

I would like to help Henry find this out as quickly as possible, to really understand what is happening with people so he can more easily find his true friends, and so he can better serve those he would like to help in this life.

TAKING LIFE

I have daydreamed of an empty world,
sifting through pocketbooks, drawers, pictures and trinkets,
guessing at your life

Living on canned goods and vitamin packets
and, as the years pass, the vitamins decay and expire
I imagine madness would overtake me
without you there
A mind, alone, filled with energy,
eventually becoming nothing
but a static "shushing" noise

I need you
To live in this world, I need you

For though I treasure the treasures and secrets
and would finally feel the degraded vindication
of confirming I knew your every thought
I cannot last alone

Yet I also cannot stay alive,
hopping from bedroom to bedroom,
looking for mementos that suit me;
these heartbeat episodes...
No one existing anywhere...
not even someone who might surprise me
while I sift through their things,
bodies now only dust and bone
But memories and "your truth"
left to preserve what I already knew

I am satisfied, comfortably crushed beneath the weight of being with you

NOTES

We need people. To exist and stay sane in this world, we need others. Energy is dissipated between two terminals. The human mind tends to build up energy and, through communication, energy can be released and discharged.

I think many people have at one time or another imagined what it would be like and how they'd feel if all other people vanished from the Earth.

You could go throw people's sock drawers and find all their secrets.

One might feel they could go through an ex's belongings, find the evidence they knew existed all along, and somehow feel vindicated. They were "right".

But without people, it would all be meaningless, and the mind would consume itself.

Better to be crushed beneath the weight of social constructs than to be alone in this world.

THE MESSAGE

Wandering time, wondering who I was
These last millennia, blank and dark
And that familiar indignation,
(from me, or someone else, or both?)
that I should even attempt to exist
and cast such a net over time

After all, I was born, I am dying
I will die
I am blood and bone
Electrical impulses in a brain
Newton's Laws come alive

Even though I have vivid dreams
that drown me in grief, and fear, and love,
of places I've never been,
and never will be again,
composed of odd pictures,
tucked into the etched grooves inside my skull,
of the green glow of radiation in a tube,
of hunting on plains on beasts not unlike horses,
of music cascading down upon a crowd like a drug

I am in no contest with Pi,
claiming infinity
while measuring closed loops

Yet, how does one peer around a corner?
And why do mathematicians rush
to make a proof that I both can
and cannot do so?

All the same, the bars draw closed
Pulled by my hand or yours, it matters little
And with final briefing, whispered words
echoing back to me in blackness
"You are naught"
Yet I am

NOTES

First stanza - invalidation can come from self, it can come from others, and it comes from everywhere when you have ideas that are too far outside "what everyone knows". If I tell someone I'm actually not a body, I'm an immortal spiritual being that creates the universe, the odds of getting agreement are quite low, and there are a huge swath of opinions that would be formed depending on who I said this to.

Second stanza - this is "what everyone knows". It is not *the* lie, but it is a lie. You are not a brain, you are not subject to Newton's Laws (unless you say you are), or the Laws of Thermo Dynamics (unless you say you are).

Side note: people worry way too much about "statements that prove themselves". I say, "the reason you're uncertain about your spiritual beingness is because you have amnesia," and you might say, "well that isn't a refutable statement because anything I say you'll simply point back to the amnesia.

But that's not why I'm making the statement.

The philosophers of this world are largely entirely interested in proof. In argument. But the crazy part of it is, if you presented them with an argument that was rock solid and proved something to them, if that proof pointed to something they didn't want to believe, they still wouldn't believe it. They would operate as they always do, and sort of hold that argument in Limbo, waiting for the day when they can think of an argument to prove it wrong.

In the realm of the spirit, the watchword is "experience", not "proof".

So instead of saying "what's your argument", the response that would show actual interest in life would be, "show me how to experience that".

End of side note.

Stanza three - just a list of some of my own personal experiences suggesting that stanza two is wrong.

Stanza four and five - these are two of my favorites, but I wrote them way too vague.

Consider this:

1. When mathematically measuring the curve of a circle, one must use Pi in the equation.

2. Pi does not repeat, it never ends, it does not perfectly measure

3. Therefore, the indication that one cannot actually turn in a circle

4. But one does turn in a circle

5. So, what gives?

The same problem exists if you put your hands two feet apart, and then keep closing the distance halfway between them over and over. If you're only closing the distance halfway, your hands should never be able to touch, yet they do.

And you could say, well, they don't really touch because there's space between the particles. My response is, yeah, but the real indication here is that motion actually shouldn't be possible at all. But it is. So what gives?

Well, one could conclude any number of things.

And, as I note, the mathematicians rush to prove things one way or the other. Or they develop quantum mechanics so they can make statements that a thing both is and isn't at the same time.

And I say…you're getting closer to the truth with quantum mechanics, but you're missing the source of it - the spiritual being, the creator. And if you just try to examine more matter, you're just going to find more matter. *shrug*

And the final stanza - noting all these pressures, science, bodies, etc., that work to invalidate the spirit. And there are jailors on both sides of the bars - my agreement with those lies pulls the bars closed, and those who don't want others talking about lives they've lived before are also too happy to help close the door as well.

And that's the end of you!

But it's not. And never can be.

I Love You

Today I found out why
I sometimes get angry with you
and why we fight

I had a tremendous moment of clarity
The whole world went suddenly quiet
And in that peacefulness, I realized
I had been living in a hurricane
of non-stop shouting my entire life

So when you said,
"Let's take a trip somewhere,"
I only heard the pain in my back,
the "no" from a client,
the "meet this deadline" from my boss

And the countless other lines of nonsense,
carefully passed down
through the family tree,
that flooded and filled my childhood
with reasons to not do things

The volume is turning back up now
This moment is passing
But I promise, I promise
I will try to listen

NOTES

I think we all have occasional moments of extreme clarity where we realize the only solution in life is to be kind, to care, to reach out, to communicate, to forgive, to allow others to live as they wish.

And then the noise in our heads turns back up.

And we go back to having opinions about all sorts of things, and opinions about every single person we know.

I wrote this during a moment of extreme clarity while on my own spiritual path. My wife and I actually basically never fight or argue. We have rare moments of tension that we sort out very quickly, but that's all.

My muse for this poem, since it was not my own marriage, was oddly enough our neighbors.

It's odd because I never actually met them. I saw him barbecuing on their deck one day. Some months later my wife told me it looks like they split up because she saw him moving out.

Another odd thing - this happened a few years before I wrote this poem, it just randomly came to mind and I started writing.

I think all of life is interconnected and time is arbitrary.

You Are Here

Recently, they've shown the universe
to be immeasurably large,
and this, they say,
may be a huge underestimation

The Earth, shown to be an atom,
in one gigantic cobweb,
in a mansion
full of gigantic cobwebs

And scientists say they have seen no evidence of
life on other planets,
and this is worrisome to some

But why should it be?
All these empty rocks and spaces,
simply abandoned playgrounds,
stories that have been finished,
played out, and overrun

Perhaps all life has collapsed
to right here,
this head of an angel's pin,
some participating, the rest watching,
munching on popcorn in deep space,
or perhaps from just over your shoulder

After all, life can never die
And while scientists scuffle,
trying to measure masses and densities,
hoping that Elder Light

will show them where they came from,
the cosmic joke
is right in front of them,
and our audience
snorts in amused dismay
over a galaxy sized
Coca-Cola

The man in the white smock
looks directly into your eyes,
denies God,
and lies awake, sleepless, wondering
if he will ever find the smallest particle

Yet all that is real is us,
perhaps collapsed
to this tiny point of life,
ready to explode again,
children running out to recess,
to all the abandoned slides, trampolines, and merry-go-rounds,
in the only Big Bang
there has ever been,
or ever will be,
the spirit of play

NOTES

"Elder Light" is a very cool postulated phenomenon. You should Google it.

When we arrive at world peace, it would be strange for a soldier to wander out of some distant jungle he was hiding in to discover a world where no one anywhere had the impulse to hate or fight.

He would be at a point of history that was probably inevitable (and which itself would eventually pass away back into war and fighting), but which would be unbelievable and feel impossible to him.

So, what if there is no life on any planet, let's say, in our galaxy.

What if there was life. And now there is not.

Well, the spirit is immortal, so it really wouldn't be all that worrisome. But it would be a very specific and odd point in galactic history.

And it may seem impossible to us.

And as for the scientist, well this is just another one of my love letters to him saying, "If you really want answers, you have to stop looking for proof, and start looking for experience."

RECOGNITION

All things culminate
Ancient friends gather again,
knowing, thou art god

NOTES

I wrote this to say hello to an old friend. We hadn't spoken in a few years, and we hadn't been all that close. But I wanted to bypass that and just recognize the spiritual nature of both of us so we could get to real conversation.

This is also a nod to Valentine Michael Smith, Robert Heinlein's main character from his book Stranger in a Strange Land.

GREECE

Monuments of invention,
 taming nature's will
From the trembling hand of man,
waters of creation spill

Treading stone slabs carved,
guiding God's universe
Rolling from the minds that plan,
unaware of passion's curse

None wanted for better life
'til those who came to Conquer's gates,
felling the Tree of Knowledge
with such swift sword that only takes

Any man dared fight that day
protected no idea nor piece of land
Sought solace for creator woman only,
the muse and wellspring of every man

So when I take knee and vow,
forsaking all from now 'til forever's dawn,
it is I who seek the dreams of you,
to make whole once more my heart's true song

NOTES

I wrote this when I was consumed by a type of love that I now find unhealthy.

However, I do still love the poem.

I don't normally write poems that rhyme. I think this is one of two.

"Conquer's gates" is just a place where men decide they must attack; a conceptualization of "conquer" turned into a noun to represent any place men feel they must conquer.

And "such swift sword that only takes" is just a line I like that indicates that war is only destructive and destroys "the Tree of Knowledge".

This poem is also an ode to the creativity of humanity, and to the more spiritual roles of men and women in relation to each other.

OUR TRIALS

I imagine futures
These imaginations are alive and fluid

They change
I set in action toward them
and the universe interposes as a game

I slow down, I stumble, I forget,
and I re-imagine

And sometimes the imagining has changed,
and that is okay

So I set a course of action,
and what I've found
(and this has been key for me)
is that often the paths that open,
or that I discover through chance,
or help from a friend,
or just sheer surprise,
were not paths I'd thought of

Not shockingly different,
just not conceived

And so the course of action has to be adjusted,
and sometimes the imaginings change,
because everything is alive and fluid

And we change

NOTES

I wrote this just a series of thoughts and steps for a friend. They were working to create their future and asked for some perspective.

I think people sometimes get caught up in worrying about how things will end up, that it must end up exactly as they imagine or they've lost somehow. Or something takes longer. Or they have a setback.

My life has largely been based around setting off in a direction, and then finding out what happens along the way.

The keys for me in life have been:

- I have a particularly strong persistence on a given course.

- I don't worry about losses along the way, they're irrelevant and just a way to get worked up and emotional; I generally move on from them almost instantly when they happen (and they do happen).

- I am totally willing to change while on the path of persistence, but I will always be heading toward my goal.

- I know I may never reach my goal in this life; it's the path and the persistence that are what's important.

So, by all means, a person should have all the emotions they want to have. But if a person has *unwanted* emotions about the game they're playing, consider the above.

Because, in my opinion, you can never lose.

PRAYER

Each dream becomes true
Each responsibility, fulfilled
Each love blooms, ever-growing

I pray
I dream
I live

NOTES

I wrote this for myself one morning to help start my day off with the right viewpoint. It was a good day (as are most).

Also, I think the concepts of "duty" and "responsibility" are shunned too much in the world of poetry. Awareness of what they are, and growth in them, is absolutely key to a fulfilled life.

Giving Thanks

When I wake up
I want to hear my son's voice,
feel my wife's hand on my chest,
feel a winter-cold house,
smell new coffee in the air

Have nothing to do
but talk, take walks, and play,
live in a morning's autumn gray,
a winter's noon day sun

Today there is tragedy and loss,
goals grind to a halt, metal on metal,
and lives are filled with windless seas

And by these contrasts and reflections
I am filled with gratitude

NOTES

These are the things I enjoy the most, so I wrote them down on a Thanksgiving day.

Some mentors and life coaches will tell you not to compare your life to that of those less fortunate because they conceive that doing so is just a way to lessen the pressure of one's own failures to achieve one's ambitions.

There may be truth to that.

But I think it's good to give thanks, and in reflecting on those who are less fortunate, I feel we can keep our attention on the mission of life - to help others.

THE BACK 40

I stood at the watershed
in a state of harmonic
vibrant rainbow

No answers left for anything,
questions holding no meaning,
paralyzed with love

Existing only with a static
endless "whush"
of a finally empty mind

Perceiving a hollow world
filled with prismatic illusions,
my friends, myself

Each of us writhing,
gnashing, spiteful, joyful,
then finally motionless

Lying still on an improv stage
giving the performance
of a lifetime

NOTES

I'm 47 years old as of this writing.

Until the age of 35, I floated around from construction jobs, jobs making pizza, landscaping, simple office admin jobs, and babysitting.

Then, by luck, I fell into what would become my career in sales.

For my first 35 years, I simply enjoyed.

For the last 12 years, I've really started to learn.

So now, at possibly the midway point of life, I've experienced some pangs of what might be called a mid-life crisis, ennui, self-reflection, and a lot of appreciation for the things I have, the things I've done, my friend, my family, and the experience of being alive.

If I was not on the spiritual path I'm on, I think my recycle bin might be full of empty bottles of red wine. I have a lot more empathy for the human race than I did when I was younger.

But, fortunately for me, my spiritual path has brought me to experiences and understandings so profound, that I feel exterior to life much of the time, and these famous words from Shakespeare's "As You Like It" seem to contain a most profound truth.

"All the world's a stage, and all the men and women merely players. They have their exits and their entrances; And one man in his time plays many parts."

DOWN THE LINE

If I could do anything
I would play sandlot baseball
almost every day, all day
Other days, I would go bowling,
or go to the arcade
That would be Spring and Summer

In the Fall and Winter
I would drive around to small towns
and take slow walks there,
looking closely at things,
wondering at the humanity found there
Maybe once a month
I would drive to the mountains with friends
to sled in the snow

In the deeper part of winter,
those days when you go to work when it's dark,
and come home when it's dark,
one twelfth of your life when you never see the sun,
I would read books at home,
never changing from pajamas
until I had cabin fever
And then I would send a thankful prayer
to the god of cabin fever

I feel like I would chop wood,
That I should tend a garden
That eggs from chickens
and a small plot of vegetables
would be enough

That I could have quiet conversations
with acquaintance neighbors
And we would trade advices on living
And there would be lulls in the conversation,
not uncomfortable,
until one departed
as the night got cold

NOTES

Any game can be made to feel like it is important.

People literally have been murdered for performing poorly in football (soccer).

I have always loved the dichotomy show in Start Trek: The Next Generation between Jean Luc's life on a starship, and his life when he returns to Earth for short stints at his family's vineyard.

His life on the starship is fully surrounded by and run with technology.

But his life on Earth, well, that's the one I find most beautiful.

The society is "post scarcity". They have replicators that can not only create food, but can also create any building material, or basically literally any material thing programmed into it.

So this immediately reduces the challenges of life to almost nil.

However, that's not how people work, that's not how the spirit works.

The individual, the spirit, the person, requires a game. It requires the feeling of risk, the potential of failure, and the possibility of accomplishment.

And it will require that no matter how many barriers you remove from its path.

So take away the problems of food, shelter, health, etc. Take them all away. But, despite that, the spirit will find a game with risk.

It will even simply say - "sandlot baseball has risk", and then it will invent the risk.

What risk? How about "reputation in the neighborhood"? How about "looking good in front of the girl"? How about "gotta find a way to strike out Hammerin' Hank"?

And it will assign dire importance to these games. It will feel immense failure when Hank, once again, hits one over the fence.

So while this poem is about an idyllic life, a simple existence and experience, my intention was that it also has hidden in it the art, the game, and the "risk it all" experience of life as well, buried in each one of us.

Dynamic 9

Spin in
Begin

The original beingness of our dawn,
lost as we tassel down through eons

Twisting together, eyes like fire,
our only passion to create our desires

We skate vast oceans of sea-green glass,
and ponder our creation from the endless past

I saw you there, the crystal queen,
austere, at peace, the perfect ring

I came from you to start a game
You looked at me and said name

And from your mouth there came a pulse
I could not withstand and did convulse

You gave a wondering glance

Spin in again
Begin again

We danced in the ether crossing breadth and width,
constellations of laughter creating myth

The perfect coil, the untamed machine
The fount, the vessel, without a seam

Shrug and tug, push and pull,
descending from grace in a delicate lull

Down into the universe's core,
the first viewpoint of dimension we did explore

Seeing from that point of view
was cause for us to start anew

And that was when the stars fell down,
a diamond cascade of your crashing crown

Your eyes glowed red and I could not see,
blinding, ending, no recovery

You glanced about uncertainly

Spin in again
Begin again

I looked out across the twisted flow
of grass and trees that spread below

and saw you had come once more to create
the sea green glass in different shapes

The forest did change from living life
to gems of green catching the sunlight

The burning glow of your inner core
laid bare the mystery of the jungle floor

The crystal queen, now more opaque,
did not but cause my heart to break

For as I approached her garden to laud her,
my disruption did awake her ardor

Her crystal magnified my dust and mud,
and every shard did then draw blood

Your anger was a surging flood

Spin in again
Begin again

I wondered then at my new wings,
leathery and hard, covering a span most terrifying

The earth and sky were both my own
Any place I could think I was free to roam

With ease I would tear tree from earth,
buffet a cloud 'til it disbursed

Felling forests beneath fire and ash,
the sea green emerald seared to black

Animal, plant, insect consumed,
boiling rivers to slake my thirst and then resume

Copper skin and silver blue eyes,
a living eclipse wheeling in the sky

But I heard your song adrift in the warm breeze
and came to slumber, hibernate through the centuries

Your lips smiled around a melody

Spin in again
Begin again

I laughed aloud to see you again
But laughs and roars sound much the same

Of all you had built, the multitude,
they could not agree and so forgot about you

So you smashed their Babel Tower and made them forget
that they could have understanding, a scholar's regret

But the artist William Blake could still see,
pulled from myth and scripture he painted you and me

With your crown and soul of golden hue,
my skin a burnt dark copper and eyes of blue

His apocalyptic vision of a world undone,
of the Great Red Dragon and the Woman Clothed with the Sun

Devil and angel whirling in a dance of jade swords and grace,
and all mankind hurled into space

You shed a tear and looked away

Spin in again
Begin again

Now a sliver of what you once were
Survival is now a fight on death's open door

Chess pieces ready and at your disposal,
moved against your adversary in a fight for control

But the tide rolls in and the sea resounds
Unrelenting, the game reduces your shores as it pounds

And your group who seek only answers of truth
find little but spear and nail and tooth

The game is intense, your mortality close,
and the world calls for you to give up the ghost

Yet your people are like the very earth,
life has hammered them, tempering them from birth

But like all songs along a dwindling spiral,
beauty is matched by brevity and a funeral pyre

The embers of your eyes flicker-fire

Spin in again
Begin again

Housed by a mother with eyes of jade,
from the fashioning of two rings your body was made

Into a house of smooth, dark wood,
brought to a family whose lives were good

The game now reduced to a few grains of sand
So much ability lost from your command

And the soul so harbored amidst comfort and love,
conceived all large games were played by others far above

A soul's respite, a breath of vacation,
vision quite hidden by mind's machination

But war with one's brother can bring about an evolution,
and together we set out to find the solution

Perhaps you remember me from long before,
my copper skin and blue eyes standing at your mind's open door

At last, you're looking once more

Key out!
Who are you?

Now all that's left is you again
No spinning in or beginning again

And though this may at first confuse
as you look at your history and carefully peruse

All your wars and all your games,
your name renowned, your name defamed

But look beyond all your own tombs
and see yourself standing alone with your white plume

And remember when you're further down the track,
if you're missing me while you are looking back,

you can create me again to play a game,
and you can know that I will always do the same

And all our spinning is just a simple dance,
for we created everything here, every circumstance

I can see you now
End game

All that remains
is Dynamic 9
The summation of this game
containing all along the timeline

It is all wins and losses,
All knowingness and not
It is mystery and serenity,
all remember and forgot

To try to sum it up
would be to feel the universe's seams and threads
For if you can know all,
you know you're at the end

And anyhow, no word or symbol
can solve Dynamic 9
For it is the aesthetic,
so now end comm, end time

for Rhema Folk on her birthday
April 10th, 2003

www.ingramcontent.com/pod-product-compliance
Lightning Source LLC
Chambersburg PA
CBHW031305130726
47988CB00007B/2733